LEADERS LIK

Cathy Hughes

BY J.P. MILLER

ILLUSTRATED BY
AMANDA QUARTEY

Rourke
Educational Media

A Division of
Carson
Dellosa
Education

ROURKE'S
SCHOOL to HOME
CONNECTIONS
BEFORE AND DURING READING ACTIVITIES

Before Reading: *Building Background Knowledge and Vocabulary*

Building background knowledge can help children process new information and build upon what they already know. Before reading a book, it is important to tap into what children already know about the topic. This will help them develop their vocabulary and increase their reading comprehension.

Questions and Activities to Build Background Knowledge:

1. Look at the front cover of the book and read the title. What do you think this book will be about?
2. What do you already know about this topic?
3. Take a book walk and skim the pages. Look at the table of contents, photographs, captions, and bold words. Did these text features give you any information or predictions about what you will read in this book?

Vocabulary: *Vocabulary Is Key to Reading Comprehension*

Use the following directions to prompt a conversation about each word.

- Read the vocabulary words.
- What comes to mind when you see each word?
- What do you think each word means?

Vocabulary Words:	
• broadcasting	• herstory
• campaign	• maven
• communicator	• media
• format	• network

During Reading: *Reading for Meaning and Understanding*

To achieve deep comprehension of a book, children are encouraged to use close reading strategies. During reading, it is important to have children stop and make connections. These connections result in deeper analysis and understanding of a book.

 Close Reading a Text

During reading, have children stop and talk about the following:

- Any confusing parts
- Any unknown words
- Text to text, text to self, text to world connections
- The main idea in each chapter or heading

Encourage children to use context clues to determine the meaning of any unknown words. These strategies will help children learn to analyze the text more thoroughly as they read.

When you are finished reading this book, turn to the next-to-last page for **Text-Dependent Questions** and an **Extension Activity**.

TABLE OF CONTENTS

Do you have an ear for music? Are you a great speaker? Would you like to work in radio or television? Cathy Hughes is a great **communicator**. She is a leader in **media**.

Famous people walked the red carpet. They were stopped and asked questions. They were there to honor Cathy Hughes. Howard University in Washington, D.C. had renamed the School of Communications after her.

Cathy Hughes made her name as the founder of the Radio One **broadcasting** company. For over forty years she was the voice of Black America. She aired important news about Black America for Black Americans. Black artists could count on Cathy. She played their music when other radio stations would not.

A VISIONARY
Cathy Hughes is a visionary. By age 50, she was the founder of the largest Black-owned radio company in the United States.

Young Cathy knew she wanted to be in radio after her mom gave her a transistor radio for Christmas when she was eight. She pretended to report the news in the mirror using a toothbrush as her microphone.

Cathy told her friends and teachers she would be on the radio someday. Not everyone in her hometown of Omaha, Nebraska, believed her. In high school, her teacher sent home a note that said Cathy suffered from delusions of grandeur. That did not stop Cathy. She followed her dream.

Cathy's first job in radio was at KOWH in Omaha. In 1971, she moved to Washington, D.C. She became the general sales manager for radio station WHUR on the campus of Howard University. Cathy Hughes raised a lot of money for the school. It was her first step toward becoming a **herstory** maker.

WOL – WE OFFER LOVE

Northeast H Street was in one of the worst areas in Washington, D.C. It never healed from the race riots of the 1960s. In 1980, Cathy bought her first radio station, WOL-AM. It was located in the Georgetown district of Washington, D.C. Cathy decided to move her station to Northeast H Street. She wanted to be closer to her listeners.

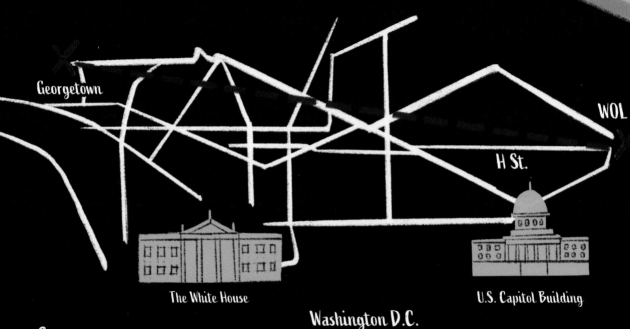

Georgetown

WOL

H St.

The White House

U.S. Capitol Building

Washington D.C.

Other business owners in the area set bars on their windows.
Not Cathy. She had a big glass window set up front.
She wanted people to see her...
trust her...
know she was there for them.

Cathy lived life by her station's name, WOL, which stood for *We Offer Love*. She wanted to make her values clear to the community.

Cathy also stepped out from behind the mic. She would go outside the station and talk to people as they passed by. She helped put on health fairs and holiday giveaways. She wanted to help the area get back on its feet.

Cathy also led the "Take it Back" **campaign**. It was directed at the *Washington Post Magazine*. She was tired of them writing only negative stories about Black people. On the air, she asked Black people to stop buying the magazine. Cathy asked that anyone who had copies of the magazine dump them on the steps of the *Washington Post*.

Thousands of copies were returned to the *Washington Post's* front door as a crowd gathered and chanted "take it back." They stopped buying the magazine for thirteen weeks until the *Washington Post* said they would commit to fair coverage. Additionally, someone from the *Washington Post* would come on Cathy's morning show once every six months.

URBAN MEDIA MAVEN

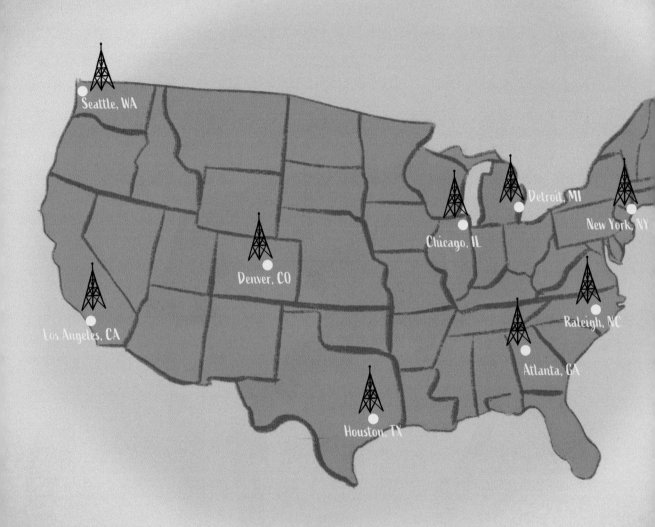

Seattle, WA

Detroit, MI

New York, NY

Chicago, IL

Denver, CO

Los Angeles, CA

Raleigh, NC

Atlanta, GA

Houston, TX

From WOL, Cathy helped the Black people of Washington, D.C. She wanted to do more. She was ready to help Black people across America.

In 1987, Cathy bought another radio station, WMMJ. As time went on, she bought more. Her radio chain became the largest Black-owned chain in the country. She named her business Radio One. With Radio One, Black people everywhere could receive the same information at the same time.

Cathy created an exciting **format**. In the mornings, she aired talk shows and guest interviews. Evenings were filled with music and entertainment.

At night, she played smooth R&B and soft jazz. She called this combination the "Quiet Storm." It was a hit. So was Radio One. In 1999, the company went public, which means that the general public could buy shares of the company.

BLACK NEWS IN AMERICA

Black people are still underrepresented in newsrooms today. Local newsrooms are still largely white. Radio One is different. Reaching 82% of Black people in America, it offers Black listeners a Black perspective.

Before long, Cathy tried her hand in television. She founded the TV One **network**. She earned the nickname "Urban Media **Maven**." Her company changed its name from Radio One to Urban One to cover the different media they were getting into.

STARS OF TV ONE
Quincy Jones, the music legend famous for producing, performing, composing, and more, was featured on TV One's hit show *Unsung*.

Cathy dreamed of a life in radio. Her faith and hard work led the way. In 2010, she was inducted into the Radio Hall of Fame.

Cathy has been honored across the country for her contributions to society. Cathy continues to work for her community not only with her work in Urban One, but also through supporting education, mentoring women, and empowering minority communities.

Cathy Hughes lives in Pasadena, California. Urban One is the largest African American-owned media company in the United States.

What I want people to remember about our brand is that we made our community a lot better than it was when we started our company in 1980.

–Cathy Hughes

TIME LINE

1947   Cathy Hughes is born April 22nd in Omaha, Nebraska.

1969   Cathy Hughes begins radio career at KOWH in Omaha.

1973   Cathy Hughes becomes general sales manager of WHUR at Howard University in Washington, D.C.

1979   Cathy Hughes buys her first radio station, WOL-AM, in Washington, D.C. Radio One (known today as Urban One) is born.

1986   Cathy Hughes heads "Take it Back" campaign. A protest against the negative portrayal of Black people in the *Washington Post Magazine*.

1987   Cathy Hughes buys her second radio station, WMMJ.

1999   Radio One becomes a publicly-traded company.

2004   Cathy Hughes launches TV One, a lifestyle and entertainment television network.

2010   Cathy Hughes is inducted into the Radio Hall of Fame.

2016   Cathy Hughes is inducted into the National R&B Hall of Fame.

2016   Howard University renames its School of Communications the Cathy Hughes School of Communications.

2017   Radio One is renamed Urban One to reflect the different forms of media it encompasses.

2019   Cathy Hughes is inducted into the National Association of Broadcasters Hall of Fame.

2021   Cathy Hughes lives in Pasadena, California, and sits on the board of Urban One.

GLOSSARY

broadcasting (BRAWD-kast-ing): sending out a radio or television program to its audience

campaign (kam-PAYN): organized action in order to achieve a goal

communicator (kuh-MYOO-ni-kate-or): someone who is able to give information, news, or ideas in a skilled way

format (FOR-mat): the appearance or style of something

herstory (HUR-stur-ee): history viewed from a female or feminist perspective

maven (MAY-ven): an expert

media (MEE-dee-uh): ways of communicating with large numbers of people such as television or radio

network (NET-wurk): a group of television or radio stations in different places that broadcast the same programs at the same time

INDEX

TEXT-DEPENDENT QUESTIONS

1. Where was the first radio station Cathy Hughes worked?

2. What university named its School of Communications after Cathy Hughes?

3. What television network did Cathy Hughes start?

4. What radio program did Cathy Hughes start?

5. What did the letters WOL stand for?

EXTENSION ACTIVITY

There are many types of media. List and explain three. Choose an event in your local community, church, or school and help get the word out about the event. Which form of mass media will work best for you? Would a print source or social media post work better? Make sure that you send it out to as many people as you can.

ABOUT THE AUTHOR

J.P. Miller Growing up, J.P. Miller loved reading stories that she could become immersed in. As a writer, she enjoys doing the same for her readers. Through the gift of storytelling, she is able to bring little- and well-known people and events in African American history to life for young readers. She hopes that her stories will augment the classroom experience and inspire her readers. J.P. lives in metro Atlanta and is the author of the *Careers in the US Military* and *Black Stories Matter* series. J.P. is the winner of the 2021 Black Authors Matter Award sponsored by the National Black Book Festival.

ABOUT THE ILLUSTRATOR

Amanda Quartey Amanda lives in the UK and was born and bred in London. She has always loved to draw and has been doing so ever since she can remember. At the age of 14, she moved to Ghana and studied art in school. She later returned to the UK to study graphic design. Her artistic path deviated slightly when she studied Classics at her university. Over the years, in a bid to return to her artistic roots, Amanda has built a professional illustration portfolio and is now loving every bit of her illustration career.

© 2022 Rourke Educational Media

www.rourkeeducationalmedia.com

Quote source: TV One TV. "The Incredible Story of How 'Cathy Hughes Way' Came to Be." YouTube, October 19, 2016, www.youtube.com/watch?v=djNW04Tgyi8.

Edited by: Hailey Scragg
Illustrations by: Amanda Quartey
Cover and interior layout by: J.J. Giddings

Library of Congress PCN Data

Cathy Hughes / J.P. Miller
(Leaders Like Us)
ISBN 978-1-73165-182-2 (hard cover)
ISBN 978-1-73165-227-0 (soft cover)
ISBN 978-1-73165-197-6 (e-Book)
ISBN 978-1-73165-212-6 (ePub)
Library of Congress Control Number: 2021944517

Rourke Educational Media
Printed in the United States of America
01-3402111937